Original title:
The Sea's Quiet Wonders

Copyright © 2025 Creative Arts Management OÜ
All rights reserved.

Author: Giselle Montgomery
ISBN HARDBACK: 978-1-80587-366-2
ISBN PAPERBACK: 978-1-80587-836-0

Serene Depths Ascending

Bubbles float, what a sight,
Fish in tuxedos, oh what a fright!
A crab dances, lost in the groove,
While an octopus busts moves to improve.

Whales hum tunes, quite offbeat,
Seahorses prance, tapping their feet.
Starfish lounge, just taking it slow,
As jellyfish wiggle, putting on a show.

Colors of Dusk on Water

The sun dips low, in a splash of fun,
As surfboards wobble, everyone's on the run.
Crabs wear sunglasses, oh what a pair,
While seagulls dive, yelling, 'Let's share!'

A wave rolls in, but oh dear,
It swallows a hat, causing some fear.
Paddling kids, yelling with cheer,
A dance with the tide, a dandy sphere.

The Hidden Palette of the Shore

Shells painted bright, a rainbow surprise,
Giggles erupt as they cover their eyes.
A sandcastle with style, complete with a moat,
And a crab in a top hat, stealing the showboat.

Tidal pools glitter, like a jeweler's dream,
Shrimps hold a party, and the clams make a scene.
Sandy toes poke, with mischief in mind,
While seaweed wiggles, trying to grind.

Fantasies of the Foam

Foamy waves whisper tales of delight,
Of mermaid chases, in the moonlight.
They sparkle and shimmer, but wait a sec,
Is that a fish in a ball gown? What the heck?

Surfers tumble, land on their face,
As dolphins zoom by, keeping the pace.
A sand dollar giggles, just watching the show,
While sea turtles ponder, 'To dance or to go?'

Treasures of the Serene Blue

Fish wear tiny hats that spin,
While crabs dance a jig with a grin.
A starfish on a picnic laid,
With jellybeans, it surely played.

Seashells gossip on the shore,
And seagulls ask for snacks galore.
As dolphins jump and high-five each,
The ocean's fun is out of reach!

The Magic of Submerged Dreams

A turtle slips through bubbles bright,
Sipping tea with a fish in flight.
Octopuses juggle seashells round,
While mermaids sing with giggles sound.

Eels in bow ties wave hello,
As starry skies begin to glow.
Pufferfish puff, then burst in cheer,
Their party hats—oh dear, oh dear!

Murmurs of the Aquatic Realm

Crabs wear boots and stroll with flair,
In underwater fancy wear.
A dogfish tells a knock-knock joke,
The anemone starts to choke.

Clownfish chuckle with delight,
As bubbles float and dance in light.
A whale blows bubbles high in air,
While fish all stop to stop and stare!

Reflections on Still Water

A lily pads hosts a tea time snuggly,
With frogs in suits, they look so smugly.
Dragonflies wear shades supreme,
Sharing jokes about a dream.

With a splash, a fish takes flight,
Chatting clouds, oh what a sight!
In quiet depths, the jesters reign,
Water's laughter, always plain!

Dreams Cradled by the Ocean's Edge

A crab in a tuxedo, quite the sight,
Waltzes on sand, under moonlight.
With shells for a hat, and a grin so wide,
He calls out to fish for a dance, with pride.

Seagulls gossip like old maids at tea,
Trading tales of the deep, rambunctious and free.
They swoop down for snacks—oh what a display!
Champion of lunch, they steal fries away!

Soft Gleams of Distant Shores

Starfish sunbathe, all splayed out and tan,
Plotting their conquests with a meticulous plan.
They take a break, sipping seaweed smoothies,
Practicing poses, these beachside beauties!

A dolphin decides to join in on the fun,
Pulling off flips like he just won a run.
Splashing the folks with his grand acrobatics,
Leaving them laughing, all summery antics!

Underwater Sonatas

An octopus band plays a lively tune,
With shells and seaweed, they jam 'til noon.
A clownfish sings—off-key, full of cheer,
His bubbles pop loud, we all stop to hear.

Turtles tap dance, their shells blinking bright,
Drifting with rhythm, a marvelous sight.
They twirl past the corals, twinkling like stars,
Underwater parties, with no sign of bars!

Whispers in the Wake

The waves gossip in ripples and rolls,
Sharing secrets that wander the shoals.
A wink from a fish, a nod from the tide,
Balancing laughter with the ocean wide.

Mermaids flip their hair, in laughter they gleam,
Plotting some pranks, plotting a dream.
With giddy delight, they splash and they swirl,
Creating confusion in their watery whirl!

Whispers of the Tides

Crabs in tuxedos dance with glee,
A conch shell gossiping, 'Come see me!'
The starfish giggles, all tucked in tight,
As jellyfish float like kites in flight.

The squid tells jokes that make us squeal,
With tentacles waving, they're quite the deal.
The fish wear hats that are oh-so-bright,
While octopuses juggle with all their might.

Secrets Beneath the Waves

Sea cucumbers whisper, 'What a sight!'
While sea urchins chuckle with delight.
The barnacles brag 'We're stuck on this wave,'
As fish serenade in a colorful rave.

A turtle named Tim loves the limelight,
He dashes and splashes, oh what a fright!
The clams snap shut with a comic pout,
While dolphins spin and dance about.

Lullabies of the Ocean Floor

Doo-wop sounds from the coral band,
Singing sweet melodies, oh so grand.
A lobster croons in a shell-shaped hat,
While anemones sway, how about that?

The snails wear boots that glitter and glow,
Sailing on currents, they put on a show.
The plankton prance like they own the scene,
In the night's spotlight, they twinkle and preen.

Tranquil Currents

A crab in shades is sunbathing slow,
As seahorses twirl in a synchronized flow.
The tides tickle fish, who swim with flair,
And the water's giggle hangs sweet in the air.

With a wink and a wiggle, they start a race,
And the octopus laughs, 'I'll win this space!'
While barnacles cheer from their rocky perch,
In this lively realm, there's never a search.

Gentle Breezes and Whispered Waves

When the wind tells tales with a gentle sigh,
Seagulls gossip, and seaweed does fly.
A crab dances sideways, what a funny sight,
While fish gossip in bubbles, oh what a delight!

The pelicans plot with their feathery friends,
Sharing secrets that the ocean bends.
With each little splash and wave that breaks,
It's a comedy show that the coastline makes!

Veils of Mist Over Blue Horizons

Misty veils float like a bride in white,
While dolphins leap with pure delight.
A hermit crab's house is way too tight,
Yet he struts around like he's got it all right.

From surfboards that topple to boats that sway,
Each splash and each laugh, a playful display.
The ocean's giggles swirl in the spray,
It's a party out here—who needs a ballet?

Untold Legends from the Abyss

What secrets lie in the deep blue below?
Maybe a mermaid with a fishy show.
Or a whale with a sense of comedic flair,
Shouting punchlines into the salty air!

Octopuses sketching the quirkiest art,
Tentacles muddling, but they play the part.
The fish roll their eyes, 'Oh no, not again!'
As the eels tell the jokes—they're the funniest men!

Rhythms of the Gentle Tide

The tide comes and goes with a funny little dance,
Like a kitten who just can't find romance.
Seashells giggle as they roll on the sand,
While crabs hold a meeting, it's all quite planned!

Oh, the whispers of waves, like tickles on toes,
Make even the grumpiest fishermen doze.
With nature's rhythm, they shuffle and slide,
In this silly ballet of the gentle tide!

Songs of the Forgotten Depths

Bubbles rise like giggling fish,
A crab sings softly, what a wish.
Starfish dancing on a sandy floor,
Whispering tales of sea folklore.

Octopus plays hide and seek,
With a wiggle here, then a peek.
They swap their hats like playful jest,
In the depths where the sun can't rest.

A dolphin dreams of skyward hops,
While plankton joke, the party stops.
Eels dive deep in rubbery glee,
Chasing shadows of the bubbly sea.

With each splash, a secret shared,
Among the waves, no one is scared.
The depths are playful, like a prank,
Where even anchors give a wank.

Flickers of Light in Dark Waters

In the gloom, a shrimp does glide,
With dance moves that can't be denied.
Neon fish throw a wild ball,
While jellyfish wiggle and sprawl.

A whale hums a broken tune,
That drifts like clouds on a sunny noon.
Turtles laugh at their slow pace,
In an underwater, funny race.

Squid squirt ink like it's confetti,
Turning the ocean into a jetty.
A puffer fish puffs with pride,
While sea cucumbers giggle and hide.

A conch shell plays a seaside song,
In rhythms friendly, never wrong.
Beneath the waves, a slapstick show,
Where every current has a flow.

An Overture to the Unseen

A clownfish wears a goofy grin,
Waving hello to a spiky fin.
In the reefs, laughter echoes clear,
As fish tickle sharks, what a cheer!

The currents hum a silly tune,
While seaweed sways and shimmies soon.
Anemones pop like balloons in spring,
As crabs march on, doing their fling.

A walrus tries to breakdance fast,
But tumbles down with a splashing blast.
The corals giggle in technicolor,
While fish tease each other, saying, "Sucker!"

Seahorses waltz with a twist and turn,
Creating waves where none would learn.
In this world where oddities reign,
The unseen laughs with joyous gain.

The Ocean's Subtle Symphony

A trumpet fish blows a silly sound,
While fitfully swirling all around.
Clams keep time in a clammy beat,
Jigs and jives with their little feet.

The sea stars twinkle with fervent glee,
While mollusks hum a tune by the sea.
An orchestra of bubbles in the swirl,
As a dolphin spins like a dizzy twirl.

Coral towers join the music game,
In colors bright, they bring no shame.
Horseshoe crabs explode with flair,
Clapping claws with unique care.

From the deeps, a melody will rise,
With giggles shared under the skies.
In this world where sea creatures prance,
Harmony thrives in a watery dance.

Portraits of Undersea Serenity

Bubbles rise like tiny gnomes,
They giggle as they float on home.
Fish wear hats and dance with flair,
Shrimp take selfies with a stare.

Coral reefs throw disco balls,
Crabs moonwalk, making calls.
Anemones play hide and seek,
While clams gossip, oh so sleek.

Octopuses draw portraits grand,
With paintbrushes in their hand.
Seahorses twirl in rainbow hues,
While a starfish reads the news.

Jellyfish float, they don't take sides,
With lanterns bright, they take moon rides.
The ocean's a circus, free and bold,
Where laughter echoes, tales unfold.

Grazing the Edge of the Blue

Seagulls wear sunglasses, looking cool,
While crabs play chess beside the pool.
Starfish knit with softest threads,
They spin stories in cozy beds.

Schools of fish do synchronized spins,
Competing for gold—the sea begins.
A whale cracks jokes, a comedian grand,
While dolphins dance in a conga band.

Turtles race with a slow, sly grin,
But always lose to the currents' spin.
The sun's reflection is a ball,
And sardines make a shiny wall.

Anemones wave with fluffy cheer,
Wishing for cupcakes to appear.
The edge of blue brings smiles all day,
Oceans play tricks in a cheerful way.

The Calm and the Color of the Sea

Under the waves, there's a calm parade,
Where shrimp juggle and clams serenade.
Purple squids strum on seaweed strings,
While playful dolphins play with rings.

Fish throw parties, it's quite the scene,
With sea cucumbers dancing so keen.
A grouper jokes, telling tales of yore,
Making even the sea turtles roar.

Colors flash like neon signs,
As barnacles form a choir in lines.
A pufferfish dons a special crown,
Each giggle sends ripples all around.

Eels pop out just for the heck,
And sea urchins yell, "What the deck?"
The calm and the color blend with glee,
Creating laughter deep in the sea.

Soft Kisses of Ocean Foam

Ocean foam whispers soft and sweet,
Tickling toes, a playful treat.
Starfish winks with a cheeky grin,
Sandy crabs dance, their legs a spin.

Seashells gossip with the tide,
Sharing secrets they can't hide.
The dolphins, with a splashy flair,
Turn somersaults in salty air.

Waves crash down with a hoot and huff,
While sea turtles puff and bluff.
Murky waters hold a froggy croon,
As mermaids dance under the moon.

Jellyfish glide in glowing trails,
Sending giggles through ocean gales.
With soft kisses, the foam does tease,
Nature's laughter in ocean's breeze.

Mirrored Skies and Ocean Depths

Beneath the waves, the fish do dance,
With jellybeans that wear a pants.
The crab in slippers, oh what a sight,
Goes moonwalking under the moonlight.

A shoal of sardines forms a line,
Waiting for the punchline, oh so fine.
They giggle as they swim around,
In a bubble-blowing underwater sound.

A turtle in a tie greets the day,
With a stylish grin, he wades to play.
Seahorses giggle, caught in delight,
As they twirl in circles, what a funny sight!

And when the dolphins laugh and squirt,
They turn the ocean into a concert.
With mirthful waves and bubbly cheer,
Life beneath can be such a queer!

Illuminated Paths Below

In a sunbeam's wink, the crabs unite,
Wearing shades for the dazzling light.
A clownfish plays peek-a-boo,
Tickling an octopus, who turns blue!

The jellyfish float like balloons on a spree,
Chasing away any gloomy decree.
They pulsate and sway in a jolly way,
Announcing that it's party day!

Starfish are busy with their grand ballet,
Dancing a jig that steals the day.
With a wink and a wave, they invite a crowd,
As sea urchins cheer, slightly loud.

A starry night in water sans stress,
Turns the sea floor into a fun fest.
With laughs, splashes, and whimsical swells,
What tales the ocean's laughter tells!

The Artistry of Shoreline Silence

At low tide, the clams have a chat,
In their shells, discussions on what's up with that.
The sandpipers strut with some attitude,
Discussing the best seaside food.

A crab with a hat sings a beachy tune,
As the gulls gather 'round, dancing like loons.
They take turns sharing their best sea joke,
While a starfish giggles, "Hey, I'm no bloke!"

Seashells argue on who's the best,
But all agree, it's the tide that's blessed.
Slippers and flip-flops join in the fun,
As laughter spills over, second to none.

When the sun dips low, it's time to retire,
But the gadgets of tidepool still conspire.
Every shell tells a tale, always sublime,
The funny shore whispers, "Come back sometime!"

Aquatic Reveries at Twilight

At dusk, the sun's pink brush paints the tide,
A dolphin flips with a joyous glide.
Seagulls squawk, sharing stories so wild,
Of fishy adventures and when they were styled.

The otters get busy, cracking up laughs,
While clam chowder dreams of other half's.
They stack pebbles like pyramids tall,
Then chase them down, giggling through it all.

With laughter under stars that brightly gleam,
Starfish play cards in a tricky dream.
It's not just fish going with the flow,
Even the mullet got a show!

As night falls deep, the tides giggle and sway,
Carrying secrets of the silly sea play.
The waves whisper softly, "Till next we meet,"
In aquatic romance, oh, what a treat!

Echoes in the Coral Depths

In the reef, a fish went by,
Waving fins and shouting 'Hi!'
A turtle laughed, with quite the grin,
Said, 'Don't splash, you'll sink like sin!'

Corals giggled, colors bright,
Crabs scuttled, feeling light,
An octopus with lots of flair,
Wore a hat made of seaweed hair!

Jellyfish danced, a wobbly waltz,
Said, 'Oops, sorry, that was my fault!'
A clam then snapped, 'Keep it down!'
Or else I'll frown and wear a crown!

Echoes bubbled, laughter rang,
In underwater fun, they sang,
For in this realm of ocean cheer,
Every day is wild and dear!

A Dance of Moonlit Tides

Under the moon, the crabs all pranced,
Clumsy steps, yet they advanced,
A starfish said, 'Look at my moves!'
But fell in mud, oh how it grooved!

Mollusks twirled in pearly gowns,
The fish rolled eyes and tossed their frowns,
'Can you swim or just float there?
While I'm doing laps like I just don't care?'

Seahorses swayed with gentle grace,
But one got dizzy, lost the race,
It spun and twirled, a funny sight,
As waves applauded with delight!

The tides laughed hard, their bubbles burst,
As creatures danced, they gave their worst,
Yet laughter echoed through the night,
In moonlit joy, all felt just right!

Silent Shores at Dusk

On the shore where seagulls squawk,
A crab tried walking, what a shock!
He tripped and tumbled in the sand,
Declared, 'At least it's soft and grand!'

Seashells whispered tales of yore,
Of fish who fished and splashed ashore,
A hermit crab with quite the shell,
Said, 'Classy fashion, I wear so well!'

The sunset painted skies of gold,
While waves tickled toes, brave and bold,
A lost flip-flop floated by,
The tide just winked and said, 'Oh my!'

At dusk, the beach held laughter's song,
With quirky tales that kept folks strong,
For silent shores could make you grin,
Just humor found beneath our skin!

Harmonies of the Ocean Deep

The fish in schools sang sweet and low,
While dolphins jumped, putting on a show,
Starfish clapped in leafy beds,
Cheering loudly with their heads!

The seaweed waved, a lively crowd,
As a clownfish boasted, laughed out loud,
'Can't keep up with my fancy jig,
Don't even try, it's just too big!'

Bubbles rose like tiny tunes,
The octopus joined, danced with spoons,
Said, 'Underwater, I'm quite the sight,
With tentacles bending left and right!'

As coral reefs hummed harmonies,
Laughter echoed with the breeze,
For in this world of underwater glee,
We find our joy, wild and free!

Stillness in the Blue Abyss

In the depths where fish do nap,
A crab sings lullabies on a map.
Seahorses waltz in their fancy attire,
While jellyfish float like confetti in fire.

The octopus hides with ink and a grin,
Pretending to be a rock, quite the win!
Clownfish giggle as they swim in loops,
While prawns throw parties with buckled up troops.

A starfish dreams of being a star,
Wishing for fame and a fancy guitar.
Each wave tells tales of laughter untold,
In a world where the silly is brave and bold.

So join the fun in the liquid mist,
Where even the seaweed shakes with twist—
In this realm of bubbles and glee, oh my,
You might find joy as the fish swim by!

Shadows of the Tidepool

In pools where the tide likes to play,
There's a crab who thinks he's a ballet.
With pirouettes on the slippery floor,
He scuttles around, not a care to bore.

Sea slugs are sluggers in strange little hats,
While snails roll their eyes at the flipping spats.
Starfish toss shadows like clumsy ballerinas,
While sea cucumbers mind their own business—meaners!

Anemones wiggle in a colorful dance,
Enticing a fish with a not-so-fine chance.
But pufferfish puff up, proclaiming their might,
As seagulls stare down for a comical bite.

With laughter echoing through rocky retreats,
Turtles share jokes while holding their seats.
In the mirth of the tide and its frothy role,
The puddles of fun are a joy to behold!

Beneath the Weaving Waves

Beneath the waves where laughter is grand,
A sea otter juggles with shells in his hand.
Fish swim in circles, all giggles and gleam,
While plankton join in for a whimsical dream.

A clam wrote a letter to send to a friend,
But pearls were the postage, and that's how they spend.
Lobsters trade secrets with whispers of cheer,
Creating a ruckus whenever they near.

Dolphins play tricks, wearing wigs made of foam,
While anemones hold a fast-fashion show at home.
Each flip brings a chuckle, each dive a delight,
As barnacles chuckle throughout the night.

In this underwater land of fun so bright,
Mermaids sing songs that are silly and light.
With krill doing limbo and whales rolling by,
The ocean's a circus where fish laugh and fly!

The Calm Embrace of the Deep

In the calm waters where giggles can hide,
A seahorse gallops with pride, what a ride!
Starfish throw parties with shells for the seat,
While mermen canoodle and dance to the beat.

The turtles are gossiping, sharing old tales,
Of treasure hunts gone wrong or fish with pink scales.
A pufferfish prances with clumsy finesse,
Making all the grouper feel funny with stress.

Jellyfish jive in their floaty attire,
Poking each other, then catching the fire.
With nudibranchs dressed like disco delights,
They slide over corals, oh, what a sight!

So if you explore the calm ocean's sweep,
Where laughter and whimsy run wild and deep,
Just remember the magic that all creatures bring,
In this joyful domain where the silly will sing!

Serene Moments in the Deep

Fish in tuxedos dance with glee,
A crab complains, 'Why not me?'
The octopus wears a silly hat,
While seaweed twirls like a chatty brat.

Starfish lounges, soaking sun,
Counting its rays, it's having fun.
A clam gets fresh, slams shut with sass,
While jellyfish float, just full of class.

Mermaids giggle, flip their hair,
Dolphins leap without a care.
A sea turtle, wise and slow,
Whispers jokes that only it knows.

Bubbles rise like laughter's hum,
As the tide plays a teasing drum.
In these depths, where stories swirl,
Why not laugh and give it a twirl?

Beneath the Glistening Surface

Anemones wave like fans in cheer,
While bloated pufferfish draw near.
They puff up big, then shrink right back,
In this pool of gags, there's hardly a lack.

Mollusks gossip, stuck to their shells,
Trading tales and salty spells.
A sea cucumber tells a tall tale,
Of swimming laps without a scale.

Sea horses tango, all dressed up,
While barnacles cling, drinking from a cup.
Whales blow bubbles, not to impress,
But mostly to clean up their mess!

Snails take a stroll—what a sight!
Each inch a mile, such pure delight.
In this watery job, who needs a plan?
When every wave is a chance to stand!

Secrets of the Still Current

Eels do cartwheels, caught in the flow,
While lazy seashells just sit and glow.
A dolphin spins—a whisker of speed,
Knocking over seaweed, planting a seed.

Tangled old nets multiply their tricks,
Snagging the oddest of oceanic picks.
A fish with googly eyes that pop,
Flops on a coral, decides it won't stop.

Under the surface, a party unfolds,
Where sea cucumbers share tales of old.
They chortle and chuckle, turning quite red,
As a clam joins in, saying, "I'm fed!"

A throne made of driftwood, a crab's choice seat,
His royal decree? "Let's all eat!"
In ripples of laughter, the current does sway,
With secrets of life, come ride the spray.

Triptych of Waves and Shells

Waves giggle softly, tossing their curls,
Shells keep their stories like mischievous pearls.
A starfish stretches, begins to strut,
Saying, "Check me out; I'm the real 'nut'!"

Crabs play tag, scuttling with zest,
Dodging fisherman's nets, they're the best!
A shimmering fish joins the chase,
Performing a flip, it finds its grace.

Seagulls squawk, think they're so grand,
While a wise old turtle gives a wave of his hand.
"Don't you dare take my lovely feast,
Or I'll show you a game—what's your least?"

In ripples and roars, the fun floods the shore,
Each creature a part of the laugh's sweet encore.
Beneath the bright skies, where humor's a tide,
Join the hullabaloo, take a whimsical ride!

Beneath the Sea's Gentle Embrace

Fish wear hats made of kelp,
An octopus sings with a belt.
Sea turtles dance in a line,
While crabs do the jig, feeling fine.

Starfish gossip, all out of touch,
Counting their arms, oh so much!
A turtle drags a floating log,
Saying, 'It's my personal fog!'

Nudibranchs paint with their flair,
Spreading colors like they don't care.
A seahorse plays peek-a-boo,
While a clam plays hide and seek too.

In the coral, a party grows,
While barnacles gossip about toes.
Life's a splash, take the plunge,
Underwater fun, let's all lunge!

Lullabies of the Underwater World

A grouper hums a sleepy tune,
While sea cucumbers sway to the moon.
Sardines twirl in a dainty waltz,
"Who knocked my scales? Was it a catfish fault?"

A starry night with a glowing fish,
That dreams of being a tasty dish.
The clownfish giggle, dressed up like jesters,
In a bubble party, they're the best festers!

Anemones sway, arms all around,
While a pufferfish plots on the ground.
"Don't square dance with that crabby dude!"
Or you'll end up with tangled food!

With a salty breeze, a lullaby flows,
As a dolphin casually strikes a pose.
Mermaids laugh, their hair a mess,
In this gentle world, nothing less!

Mysterious Depths at Twilight

At dusk, the fish become quite bold,
Crabs tell tales from days of old.
A dolphin who plays with a scared old shark,
Turns the midnight into a lark.

Anglerfish flash, 'Just check my light!'
But all the clowns think it's a fright.
"Your bait's too flashy," the cod does scoff,
"Less light, more fish; just chill and scoff."

Echoes of laughter through water drift,
As squids do tricks, but not the swift.
Under moonlight, the seaweed twirls,
While jellyfish drift in stellar swirls.

In the dark, a sea otter floats,
Keeping treasures, the tinker of boats.
Nighttime giggles, a cheerful sight,
In the depths where all feels light!

Tranquil Currents of the Mind

In currents calm, ideas drift,
A fish thinks hard, giving thought a lift.
"Should I wear stripes or polka dots?"
Contemplating fashion is what he's got!

A wise old crab shares secrets deep,
While clownfish giggle, just can't keep.
They swim in circles, doing the cha-cha,
Between reef rocks, oh, what a saga!

Seahorses ponder the meaning of styles,
Talking of dreams, and goofy smiles.
"Should we parade or just float in peace?"
As they hold on tight, hoping for release.

The sea whispers softly, tales to unwind,
With bubbles of laughter, sweet and kind.
In tranquil waters, fun thoughts unwind,
Letting joy bloom in the quiet mind.

Silent Pools of Ocean Dreams

In pools so still, the fish play hide,
They giggle and splash from side to side.
A crab in a tux, he struts with flair,
Misplacing his claws, a comical scare.

Starfish chill with a laid-back grin,
Waving at dolphins, 'Come join in!'
Seashells chuckle, gossip all day,
While barnacles dance, but not in ballet.

A jellyfish floats, with a wobbly sway,
Telling grand tales of underwater play.
The rocks roll their eyes, tired of the show,
While a clownfish jokes, "I'm the best in the flow!"

And so in these pools, life's a big jest,
Each wave a punchline, nature's best quest.
So come for a dip or just watch the fun,
At the silent pools where the laughter's begun.

The Caress of Gentle Breezes

Breezes tickle with a playful tease,
Making kites dance, swooping with ease.
Seagulls complain, 'Where's my lunch, dude?'
While sand grains giggle beneath our mood.

Flip-flops chatter on a long, hot walk,
Telling tales of the great beach talk.
A squirrel steals snacks, oh what a sight,
As cooler tops close, a comical fight.

A beach ball rolls, just out of reach,
While a crab plays the world's tiniest beach.
In the shade, umbrellas hold hands so tight,
As wind whispers secrets on a warm, sunny night.

So relish the breezes, the laughter they bring,
As nature performs her lighthearted fling.
With every gust, feel the joy so bold,
In this quirky world where the breezes unfold.

Tides of Time and Tranquility

The tides come in with a lopsided grin,
Salty surprises, where do I begin?
A starfish insists, "I'm a celebrity!"
While sea cucumbers just scoff at petty.

Barnacles gossip, holding on tight,
To rocks that rumble with a ticklish delight.
The waves drop jokes as they crash on the shore,
While seashells group hug, saying, "One more!"

A surfboard's misplaced, caught in a wave,
As a seal takes a dive, oh how he misbehaves!
The tide does a jig, a slick little dance,
While seaweed winks, "Hey, give me a chance!"

So join in the fun, let the laughter flow,
In tides of amusement where time steals the show.
Each ebb and each flow, a whimsical spree,
Nature's own carnival, just you and me.

Whispers through Salty Air

Salty air carries whispers of fun,
"Hey, watch out! Here comes that bird on the run!"
With each gust, there's laughter anew,
As crabs take a bow, 'Look at me, too!'

A fisherman's hat takes off like a kite,
The ocean's too big, the fish laugh at sight.
The waves giggle softly, tickling the shore,
Inviting us all for a light-hearted tour.

Sandcastles wink, wearing shells like crowns,
While beachgoers laugh, 'We're never in frowns!'
A pirate's lost parrot, squawking a tune,
Joins in the fun beneath the bright moon.

So breathe in the whispers, let laughter play,
In the salty air where our worries drift away.
Each puff a reminder, a joke to be told,
In the playful embrace of a world bathed in gold.

Mystery at Low Tide

Where did the starfish leave its shoe?
A crab in a top hat, what shall we do?
The jellyfish giggles, floats like a kite,
Say, did you see that? They're dancing tonight!

Seaweed's a wig on a fish with flair,
A clam tells a joke, but none seem to care,
Shells play the xylophone, making a scene,
While seagulls join in, they've formed a routine!

What's that over there? A treasure, I swear!
Just a bottle with notes and a fish in despair.
With laughter abound and splashes so spry,
The tide's a comedian, oh my, oh my!

Let's gather our snacks from the sand, how quaint,
A sandwich-sized crab thinks he's an old saint.
I'll share my fries, you can have my cope,
In this comic cove, we're all fish out of hope!

Nautical Reveries

In the morning light, a dolphin does prance,
He wears a top hat – oh, what a chance!
With flippers so fancy, he takes to the stage,
While seagulls squawk loudly, they're all in a rage.

Octopuses tango, their eight legs in sync,
They whisper sweet nothings, instead of a wink.
The barnacles giggle, they're tickled by glee,
As fish in tuxedos all sip on their tea!

A pompous old turtle declares he's the king,
While the rest of us fish just vibrate and sing.
"Your crown's made of seaweed!" the shrimp starts to yell,
With laughter and bubbles, all's well in their shell.

From mackerels flying the flags of delight,
To sea cucumbers throwing a fright!
In this world beneath, where the whimsy runs deep,
We dance and we laugh till the sun makes us sleep!

Murmurs of the Coral Garden

In a garden of colors, the fish all debate,
A clownfish is grumpy about his fate.
"Why am I funny?" he shouts with disdain,
While corals are chuckling, they just can't contain!

Eels in their holes keep whispering schemes,
"Let's throw a big party!" they dream up in teams.
With sea anemones dancing in cheer,
They're planning a ball for all friends ever near!

A lionfish struts with his poisonous flair,
But no one's impressed, they simply don't care.
"Your spikes are too silly!" a flatfish then said,
And everyone giggled, as laughter soon spread!

The shrimps served some snacks from a seaweed tray,
"Who forgot the seasalt?" a clam cried in dismay.
But in the bright coral, what matters the taste,
Is the joy in the depths, where no moment's waste!

A Dance of Fathoms

Underwater lights show the dance of the fish,
A pink puffer puffs up – it's his biggest wish!
Sea turtles waltz, their elegance grand,
With dolphins doing flips, it's quite the choral band!

A seahorse in stripes thinks he's quite the charmer,
While a snail in a shell is the freshest new armor.
With bubbles like confetti, it's a grand masquerade,
The ocean floor bustling, it feels like a parade!

But who's that who tripped on an octopus' leg?
A crab with a tutu now dances a beg!
"Who knew we had clowns in these whimsical tides?"
With laughter and splashes, the whole ocean glides.

With anchors of fun, and the waves casting cheer,
All creatures involved radiate love here!
So let's dance through the fathoms, let's sway with delight,
In this wonderful water where everything's bright!

Silent Journeys Through the Blue

Bubbles rise like tiny jokes,
Fish swim by, playing folks.
Starfish giggle on the sand,
Crabs do the cha-cha, oh so grand.

Seagulls squawk, they tell a tale,
Of a fish who learned to sail.
Waves tickle toes, it's such a treat,
As hermit crabs shuffle on their feet.

A dolphin checks his sparkling grin,
While clams hold secrets deep within.
Eels wiggle with a twist and shout,
This underwater dance is no doubt!

So raise a glass of salty foam,
For all those critters in their home.
Let's share a laugh in waters wide,
Where nature plays, and joy can hide!

The Enchantment of Hidden Shores

Pebbles laugh beneath our toes,
Collecting secrets that no one knows.
Shells wear hats like silly fools,
While barnacles keep the cutest jewels.

A crab in slippers takes a stroll,
Dancing near the water's shoal.
Seaweed does a funky sway,
In the ocean's party, come what may!

Gulls wear shades, they think they're cool,
While fish parade just like in school.
Turtles slow dance with quicksand,
In this lively, ebbing band.

So treasure tales from under waves,
Where laughter lives and joy behaves.
At hidden shores, let giggles flow,
As we explore what's high and low!

Cradled by Ocean's Embrace

In swaying arms, the currents play,
Where jellyfish float like a soft ballet.
Octopuses show off their new ink,
While plankton have parties that make us think!

A starry night beneath the foam,
Where sea snails creep and call it home.
Fishies whisper tales of glee,
As they hide in rocks, just you and me!

Mermaids brush their flowing hair,
As sea cucumbers share a dare.
Coral's colors wink and shine,
Brushing off mud, feeling just fine!

So breathe in deep that salty air,
And laugh at all the jokes we share.
In every wave and splash we face,
Life's funny moments leave a trace!

The Palette of the Tide

Waves bring colors, a dreamy sight,
Brushstroke fishes darting bright.
Clams wear pearls like fancy rings,
And the ocean hums while dolphins sing.

A sandy artist with a grainy hat,
Makes castles for crabs who tip their spat.
Sea urchins poke with little pride,
While seahorses dance, a curly ride!

Tides paint stories in shades of blue,
Whispering secrets that are brand new.
With laughing gulls, the canvas flies,
In this watery world, our joy defies!

So let's dip our toes in splashes bold,
Where every wave has laughter told.
In the palette of the ocean's spree,
Let's create memories, you and me!

When the Ocean Holds Its Breath

In a moment so still, the fish just stare,
Even crabs stop their dance in the salty air.
They wonder if dolphins are hiding too,
Avoiding the squawks of a seagull or two.

Jellyfish float like balloons of zest,
While starfish claim they're better than the rest.
A clam cracks a joke, though it's stuck in its shell,
'Why don't we dare to swim? We might just repel!'

The ocean giggles—it's a ticklish place,
With sea cucumbers wearing a smiley face.
A snail on a shell says, 'Let's just relax,'
While sea urchins plot their next humorous acts.

So when all is quiet, don't you forget,
The ocean's just playing a game of roulette.
And all of its wonders are winking at you,
In a watery world that's just waiting to skew!

Calm Waters, Quiet Souls

Beneath the calm, a lobster throws a dance,
While minnows giggle, taking a chance.
The octopus ponders, with eight arms in play,
How to juggle his pickles and make them all sway.

A turtle whispers secrets to the shells,
'Why do jellyfish keep ringing my bells?'
Each wave brings laughter, a buoyant delight,
While gulls hover above, ready to take flight.

An anemone chuckles—'I'm just like a clown!'
With bright polka dots, he wears a frown.
Yet deep down he dreams of a grand red balloon,
To float in the breeze or sing a sweet tune.

So here in the depths, where calmness can reign,
The creatures are jesters, none feeling the strain.
The laughter's contagious, spread far and wide,
In water's embrace where the funny tides abide!

Secrets of the Barnacle Bay

In Barnacle Bay, the whispers are loud,
A crab wears a hat, oh what a proud crowd.
Fish gossip about their shoes made of sand,
While oysters are plotting a big bandstand.

Tides try to teach, but they slip and fall,
'We're not good at dancing; we just have a ball!'
A rogue wave shouts, 'I'm the champion here!'
But the laughter that follows is all that we hear.

Barnacles chuckle, holding on with a grin,
'We may be stuck, but we're ready to win!'
They dream of a voyage on pirate-filled seas,
With treasure of laughter and jokes if you please.

So come to the bay where the secrets unfold,
In each bubbling current, a story is told.
The giggles and chuckles are not hard to find,
In Barnacle Bay, you're sure to unwind!

Enigmas in the Ebbing Tide

As the tide pulls away, the seaweed sways low,
A seahorse hums, putting on quite the show.
A clam on the sand says, 'What's the big deal?
I'm just trying to take in the ocean's appeal!'

The crabs have a meeting; they chat and they ponder,
'What if we built a sand castle of wonder?'
While the flounder insists it's a giant facade,
'Who needs a palace? Just give me a clod!'

But wait! Is that laughter beneath the water?
A fish with a joke, 'I swear, I won't falter!'
With tales about mermaids who've lost their own shoes,
Who swim in the moonlight with fancy balloons.

So as the tide ebbs, the humor runs free,
With quirks of the ocean, just wait and see.
Each wave tells a story, a giggle nearby,
In enigmas and whimsy, the sea lets out a sigh!

Timeless Secrets Beneath the Surface

In the deep, a fish wore a hat,
Said it helped him chat with a cat.
Mermaids giggled with glee,
Who knew they liked tea, just like that?

A crab danced, with shoes oh-so-new,
Twisting and turning in quite a view.
He slipped and he fell,
But all could tell,
He laughed it off like a pro would do.

A turtle in shades, quite the sight,
Sunk down for a nap through the night.
Woke up with a fright,
Thought it was daylight,
But it was just a fish throwing light.

So if you swim where the bubbles play,
Expect the odd dance or a fish ballet.
For down below,
Laughter will flow,
In ways that will surely amaze.

Serenade of the Rising Tide

When waves rise up to sing their tune,
The starfish jives to a bubbly croon.
Clams clap their shells,
While seaweed yells,
"Come dance with us under the bright moon!"

A seagull in tux, quite out of place,
Danced with a crab, a real slow grace.
With each little step,
He tripped with a rep,
But he winked, still proud of his pace!

The jellyfish float with a vibrant flair,
While fish in bow ties glide through the air.
Bubbles burst bright,
In the soft twilight,
It's a party they're eager to share.

As the tide rolls back, bringing smiles galore,
Creatures will chuckle, and a crab will snore.
With laughter and cheer,
The end is near,
But stay tuned for joy in the ocean's core!

Echoes of the Deep Blue

In shadows below, a whale told a joke,
But fish laughed too hard; he nearly choked.
"Why did the ray,
Cross the bay?"
"Because he heard there was seaweed to poke!"

Ghostly shrimp with their fleeting glow,
Sipped on the secrets the currents flow.
They whispered of tales,
With nautical gales,
And frolicked through depths, all aglow.

An octopus dressed like a hipster chic,
Served coffee to friends with a playful squeak.
"Two shots, hold the foam!
And don't you roam,
Without trying my scones, they're unique!"

So join in the fun, hear the laughter swell,
For down in the blue, they've stories to tell.
With whimsy and wit,
They show us a bit,
Of magic that's found where they dwell.

Patterns in the Sand

Footprints from fish mark patterns so neat,
While crabs make a maze with their little feet.
Seashells convene,
To play hide and seek,
Cracking up over their salty retreat.

A seagull strolls with an air of delight,
Gazing at snacks that drift down in sight.
He dives for a thrill,
Only to spill,
His lunch in the surf on a wave of fright.

Sandcastles sprout with a flourish, a plume,
With turrets and towers, who knew they'd bloom?
But a wave just can't wait,
And does all it takes,
To wash them away with a loud boom!

With treasures at hand, the tide takes its stand,
As laughter fills air, in this playful land.
So come take a chance,
Join the dance,
Where humor is scribed in the grains of sand.

The Ocean's Hidden Stories

Bubbles rise from depths unknown,
Fishy tales of mischief grown.
Crabs with hats and shells so bright,
Swim in circles, what a sight!

A dolphin's laugh, a seaweed dance,
With every wave, they take a chance.
Octopus plays cards with a grin,
While starfish tries to find a twin.

Whales compose their symphony,
Creating tunes of jubilee.
A pirate's parrot whispers low,
"Who stole my treasure? Who would know?"

So step aboard this quirky lore,
A world where giggles galore.
Where water's mystery spins its tale,
With each splash, a new detail.

Enigmas of the Deep Blue

Down below where shadows creep,
Mermaids giggle, lost in sleep.
Turtles in sunglasses take their stroll,
Waving hello, they've got soul!

Blowfish puffing just for show,
Underwater circus, who could know?
Anemones play hide and seek,
Jellyfish throw a disco peak!

A walrus winks with silly flair,
And whispers secrets to the air.
The squids, they read their daily press,
Making sure to do their best!

Each wave a secret, each splash a joke,
Where laughter dances, and silence broke.
In this blue maze, laughter flows,
With fishy tales and friend-filled shows.

Soft Shadows on Sandy Floors

Footprints dancin' on the shore,
But crabs just scuttle; who needs more?
Sandcastles teeter in the breeze,
While sea gulls plot to steal some cheese!

A starfish flops, flat as a board,
While shells negotiate, feeling adored.
Pelicans dive and come up wet,
Swapping confessions, a grand duet!

A tiny shrimp with biggest dreams,
Dances in snickers and silly gleams.
Waves tickle toes and laughter bursts,
Making the shore where joy immerses.

With sandy toes and salty hair,
Funny antics dance in the air.
In this coastal playground, we play,
Where shadowy laughs brighten the day.

The Calm Before the Storm

Whispers ride on the ocean's sigh,
As seagulls gossip and say goodbye.
Waves in silence, with a twist of fate,
Fish hold meetings, they can't be late!

A crab prepares with a tiny broom,
Saying, "Better clean before the boom!"
Tides draw maps in secret lines,
While barnacles share their best designs.

Clouds roll in with an easy jaunt,
Parrots squawk; it's quite the haunt.
Yet under calm, hilarity swells,
With dolphins spinning their shimmering spells!

Then a splash—oh! What's that sound?
The fun begins when chaos is found.
But for now, we float, caught in giggles,
As nature's whimsy subtly wiggles!

A Canvas of Soft Hues

Oh look at that crab with a tiny hat,
It struts on the sand, just imagine that!
A jellyfish spins in its own little dance,
Wobbling along, it's got quite a chance.

Seashells line up like they're waiting for lunch,
Each one a plate, but none seem to munch.
The seaweed is waving, it's quite the charade,
While fish play peek-a-boo in a turquoise parade.

A seagull steals fries, what a cheeky old bird,
In this sandy buffet, it seems quite absurd.
The tide rolls in, and the laughter's contagious,
As the waves tickle toes, it's truly outrageous.

Underwater rocks gossip with a soft splash,
While a clownfish winks—oh, what a brash clash!
Sea cucumbers lounge in their fancy attire,
While everyone floats, so light and merry, quite the choir!

Dreaming in Aquatic Abyss

In dreams of fins and sparkling scales,
A fish tells tales with giddy details.
There's a whale who hums in a velvet chair,
While crabs crack jokes without any care.

A turtle in shades rides the current so slick,
While dolphins are plotting their next little trick.
"Oh look, there's a mermaid with a bubblegum crown,
She's trading in stories for some lost golden clown!"

Clams throw a party with glittery shells,
While shrimps do the hustle with giggles and yells.
An octopus juggles, all colors and flair,
He's quite the performer with arms in the air!

Gliding along, there's a jazzy old eel,
It boogies and wiggles, you've got to feel!
As fish play their trumpets in a joyous refrain,
Underwater dreams bring humor, never pain.

Murmurs of Sandy Shores

A starfish is sneezing—how could it be real?
With its cozy little arms, such a comical feel.
Sand dollars giggle when nobody's near,
While sea urchins hide, their spines full of cheer.

Crabs hold a seminar on walking in style,
Each with their own moves, they walk a whole mile.
The tide brings in treasures, like sandals and cans,
While tiny fish grumble, "Well, where are our plans?"

A pelican thinks it's a court jester, you see,
Dropping fish for a laugh—oh, what a decree!
The waves whisper secrets to shells on the ground,
As gurgles and glimmers make fun all around.

Drifting along, a rubber duck tagged,
Is king of the beach, oh how he brags!
The sun wears shades in its glaring delight,
Making memories under the umbrella's light!

The Dance of Light and Water

The sun does a twirl, but a cloud steps in,
Saying, "Excuse me there, let the mischief begin!"
Fish flicker their tails in a sparkling show,
While seaweed waves hello with a flowy "hello!"

A crab in a tux plays the maracas with glee,
While shoals of sardines swim chaotically free.
The tide plays a trumpet, a mesmerizing beat,
As seagulls flock in, tapping their feet.

The clowns of the ocean are putting on plays,
While squids squirt ink to add in some sprays.
A couple of lobsters, dressed up for a ball,
Are cutting a rug with their pincers so tall!

Light dances like bubbles, laughter everywhere,
With giggles and splashes, it's all in the air.
In this playful realm where joy does abound,
The whims of the water make laughter resound!

Celestial Tales of the Ocean

A starfish wearing glasses, quite chic,
Is reading a book, oh what a freak!
The dolphins dance with grace and style,
While the octopus winks with a sly smile.

Clams throw parties, they're quite the hosts,
Inviting the seaweed, they all make toasts.
Fish in tuxedos swim through the rig,
While jellyfish DJ keeps it all big!

A crab jokes loudly, he's quite the clown,
With pinchers raised high, he won't back down.
The shimmering pearls roll their eyes,
As barnacles laugh, what a surprise!

So dive in and join this underwater play,
Where laughter bubbles, brightening the day.
For in this blue realm, so silly and grand,
The ocean's delights are always at hand.

Beneath the Surface: A Veiled Journey

A turtle with shades takes a stroll on the tide,
While a schools of fish form a conga line wide.
Anemones giggle as bubbles pop out,
While the sea's silly crabs dance about.

Seahorses whisper their gossip so bold,
About a fish who is quite full of gold.
Mollusks all snicker, their shells held so tight,
While a dolphin attempts to take flight!

The jellyfish can't stop, their tentacles sway,
In synchronized moves, they're leading the fray.
A clownfish laughs, "Oh what a sight!"
As he juggles seaweed till the fall of night.

Beneath the vast blue, chaos so bright,
Creatures in currents spin left and right.
Join in the fun, don't miss the big show,
Where bubbles are laughter, and joy's set to flow.

Illusions in Aqua

With goggles and fins, the fish takes a plunge,
But a mermaid's wig makes him stop in a grunge.
"Is that real or fake?" he scratches his head,
While crabs gather round, they all want to thread.

A starfish declares, "I'm an actual star,"
While a wise old whale claims he's traveled quite far.
The seaweed sways to a funky new beat,
As snails form a band, on shells they compete!

An octopus dressed as a pirate so bold,
Steals seashells for treasure, or so he is told.
With a flip and a roll, he swipes them away,
While guppies all giggle—"Oh, what a day!"

So come peek below, where the humor is grand,
In this watery realm, it's all underhand.
From bubbles to laughter, the tales never cease,
In illusions of aqua, find joy and peace!

Murmuring Waves at Midnight

At midnight, the waves whisper secrets and jokes,
While otters play poker, breaking the strokes.
A seagull can't sing, so he hums offbeat,
While starfish tell stories, now isn't that neat?

The moonbeam shines down with a glimmering grin,
Chasing waves off to see where trouble begins.
A hermit crab shouts, "I'm the king of this shore!"
As clams with their shells declare, "We want more!"

Mermadic laughter floats soft on the breeze,
While shrimp in tuxedos dance just to tease.
The night holds a charm, a raucous delight,
With each splash and giggle, all feels just right.

So linger a moment, where tides laugh and play,
In the kingdom of water, where night turns to day.
Murmuring waves sing to keep spirits high,
Where jesters in gills make you giggle and sigh.

The Stillness of Distant Horizons

A crab in a tux, doing his dance,
Winks at the fish, takes a chance.
A seagull steals fries, oh what a sight,
As waves giggle softly, day turns to night.

The mermaid forgot where she parked her shell,
She dreams of a sparkly cocktail as well.
Jellyfish float by, looking quite grand,
But watch your toes, they don't understand!

The lifeguard's knot got stuck in his hair,
While dolphins are laughing without a care.
Sandcastles wobble, as kids run and scream,
The tide rolls in gently, spoiling their dream.

Under the sun, there's a festival breeze,
While seagulls are plotting, if you please.
A clam pulls a joke, but no one can hear,
As the ocean keeps chuckling, it's all quite clear.

Tranquility in the Brine

A fish in a bow tie, sipping on tea,
Says, "Life's quite grand with a view like me!"
Octopuses juggle shells with flair,
While crabs kick back without a care.

The sand's having a party, no shoes, just toes,
While sea cucumbers gossip about their woes.
A lobster brings snacks, all dressed in red,
But a shrimp tries to dance, and lands on his head!

Stars twinkle softly as the tide rolls away,
While fish fish for compliments, come what may.
A turtle's slow crawl, like a grand-chase scene,
In the humorous depths of the brine so serene.

The children build towers, a fortress of sand,
But the tide's got a plan, isn't that grand?
With giggles and splashes, the day marches on,
As seaweed does the cha-cha, til the dusk has drawn.

Whispers Beneath the Waves

Beneath the blue, where whispers swirl,
A fish tells a secret, gives it a twirl.
The sea sponges giggle, all covered in fuzz,
While a clam in the corner just shrugs and "buzzes."

A dolphin wears glasses, looks quite dapper,
His jokes come in bubbles—oh, what a mapper!
The shrimp took a selfie, but it came out a blur,
How do you pose with a big, wiggly fur?

A turtle's on TikTok doing the cha-cha,
While barnacles cheer, like "Ooh la la!"
Seaweed streamers wave, a festive display,
While the ocean holds laughter, in a whimsical way.

Oh, what a hullabaloo in the briny deep,
With creatures at play, it's a giggle to keep.
As waves brush the shore, the fun never ends,
And the laughter of fish, all twists and bends.

Secrets of the Tidal Realm

In a world of bubbles, the fishes conspire,
To tell the grand tales, never to tire.
A pirate crab struts, with a hat on his head,
Declaring his treasure is stale bread!

The whispering waves have secrets to spill,
As barnacles dream of a jellyfish thrill.
An eel in a tux shows up quite late,
Says, "I'm fashionably underwater, mate!"

The starfish take selfies, perfecting their pose,
While plankton are dancing in ruffled old clothes.
A clam sings out loudly, but no one will clap,
They're too busy laughing and taking a nap.

With seashells for chairs and sea foam for drinks,
The tides throw a party; what do you think?
As laughter erupts from every blue nook,
The ocean holds secrets like a curious book.

Reflections in Saltwater

Waves dance like they've lost a bet,
A crab doing the cha-cha, don't you fret!
Fish gossip in bubbles, what a sight,
While seagulls swoop down, ready to bite.

Jellyfish jellyfishing, looking quite grand,
Flipping like pancakes, all part of the plan.
Starfish just lounge, striking a pose,
That's how they roll, when nobody goes.

Sandcastles crumble at each crashing wave,
Where's the knight? Oh wait, it's just Dave!
Seashells giggle, they're wearing a grin,
As the tide pulls back, let the folly begin!

A dolphin's high five, just missed the boat,
Turns into a surf with a loud, silly gloat.
Plankton party starts as the sun starts to set,
Who knew the ocean could make us all sweat?

The Silent Symphony of Shells

In each little shell, there's a tale to tell,
Of fish in tuxedos and crabs who fell.
They sit on the sand, all polished and bright,
Like old folks at bingo, with stories in sight.

Conch shells are horns, they blow tunes quite loud,
While tiny shrimp dance, stealing the crowd.
A clam cracks a joke, but won't take a bet,
As seaweed giggles, all tangled in debt.

Oysters debate what's the best pearl,
While anemones sway, giving a twirl.
The ocean's a stage, with casts that are quirky,
Who needs a script when it's all kind of murky?

Sand dollars plot in a meeting so hush,
What's next on the agenda, a big underwater rush?
With laughter and bubbles, we toast to our friends,
In this salty realm where the fun never ends.

Beneath the Moonlit Surface

Under the moon, the fish throw a bash,
With glow-in-the-dark friends, they cut quite the dash.
An octopus juggles, with magic so grand,
While turtles just waltz, oh, isn't this planned?

Seaweed sways gently, quite lost in the groove,
While mermaids are dancing, they've really got moves.
A whale takes a dive, with a splash and a cheer,
"Did you see that?" it blubbers, "Best dive of the year!"

Starfish tell stories that tickle the sand,
Of treasure chests filled with a diary so bland.
"Do not disturb," states a clam with a frown,
While the fish make a scene, saying "Let's clown around!"

The night wears a blanket, a twinkling delight,
As bubbles rise up, in a dance of pure light.
With laughter and joy, we drift into dreams,
In the ocean's embrace, all is not what it seems.

Echoes of an Underwater Dream

Within the blue, where the silliness flows,
The fish wear top hats, striking silly poses.
Squids throw confetti, all colors that gleam,
While the ocean hums low, "Join us in this dream."

Snapper keeps snapping, the cameras, they're out,
As dolphins start flipping to uproarious shout.
"Did you see my backflip?" one dolphin will beam,
While barnacles giggle at their wacky scheme.

Crabs in a circle, they're playing charades,
With gestures so grand, nobody's afraid.
Anemones cheer, doing the underwater jig,
While sea cucumbers laugh, not caring how big!

With every splash, a new giggle ignites,
As fishes tell tales of their fabulous nights.
In this underwater world, joyous and supreme,
We find that the best fun is lived in a dream.

Shadows Among Sea Grass

In sea grass fields, a crab does dance,
With a sideways shuffle and a funny glance.
He thinks he's a star in a little parade,
While fish roll their eyes and keep serenade.

A turtle with style, wearing a shell so loud,
Waves to a dolphin who's trying to crowd.
They giggle and splash, making quite the fuss,
While seaweed just sways, saying, 'What's the rush?'

A clam tells a tale of a shipwrecked guy,
With treasures and trinkets that caught his eye.
But all that was found was a long-lost shoe,
And a fork that he claims was his very first 'too.'

The shadows play tricks in the warm ocean light,
As eels play hide and seek, what a comical sight!
With laughter beneath, in an underwater spree,
Where whimsy and mirth are as free as the sea.

Tranquil Travelers of the Deep

A pufferfish puffs, he's a sight to behold,
Trying to impress with his stories of old.
He claims he's a knight in a bubble of pride,
While the angelfish chuckle and roll with the tide.

A jellyfish floats, with a shimmering grin,
Says, 'Watch me dance, while you try to swim!'
With each little jig, he giggles so bright,
As the shrimp hide behind, laughing out of sight.

Octopuses argue about the best ink,
One says, 'It's black!' while another says, 'Pink!'
They scribble their thoughts on a large sandy page,
And laugh as their creations become quite the rage.

As travelers roam in a world full of cheer,
They trade wacky tales as they swim without fear.
Each splash brings a giggle, a memory to keep,
In the tranquil depths where hilarity leaps.

Stories Carried by Currents

A clam writes postcards to fish far and wide,
With tales from the tide and a grin full of pride.
Each letter he sends is wrapped in a shell,
As the surf brings back giggles, oh, isn't it swell?

The currents flow fast with whispers of cheer,
Carrying tales of a lost rubber deer.
It floated for ages, on its wobbly quest,
Now it dreams of adventures with fish in a jest.

A school of bold fish sets out on the roam,
In search of the secrets of bubbles and foam.
With laughter and chatter, they swirl in a whirl,
While a wise old sea turtle's watching, with pearl.

These stories unfold as the ocean waves play,
With echoes of laughter that dance in the spray.
So swim with a smile, let your worries all part,
For the currents of joy flow right from the heart.

Melodies of the Ocean Floor

Clinking shells together, a band starts to play,
With sea cucumbers joining in their own way.
Each note skims the surface like bubbles of fun,
While squids add a beat with their ink-making run.

A starfish sits proudly, tapping out a beat,
As anemones sway, just moving their feet.
They sing of the tides, in a silly parade,
Where no one can tell if they're wiggling or laid.

A conch shell whispers secrets to the reef,
While clownfish giggle, sharing tales beyond belief.
'Have you heard of the time when a jelly lost sway?'
It tumbled and tumbled, then danced on a stray!

Thus melodies echo through currents and waves,
In a symphony played by the quirkiest knaves.
With laughter and friendships melded at the core,
The ocean's true magic unfolds evermore.

Celestial Reflections in Saltwater

The fish in tuxedos prance with glee,
Waltzing with jellyfish, oh what a spree!
Starfish hold meetings with crabs on the sand,
Debating the best way to build a grand band.

Seagulls in tuxes lend a keen eye,
Making bets on the best way to fly.
With a splash and a dash, they join in the fun,
Drifting on waves, their antics weigh a ton!

Under the waves, there's a vibrant swing,
Clams play the music, and seaweed's the string.
The octopus juggles while sea cucumbers cheer,
Life underwater is just so sincere!

Bubbles are laughter, and tides bring the joy,
Every splash a good joke, oh what a ploy!
So raise your glass high to this watery charm,
With smiles all around, who's left to disarm?

Whims of the Coastal Breeze

A seagull named Larry likes to sneak fries,
He swoops from the sky with a devilish guise.
The beachgoers laugh as he swipes and he dives,
As sandcastles tumble while Larry survives!

The wind whispers secrets to kites in the air,
With jokes about sand and a funny despair.
Beach balls are bouncing like playful young pups,
As waves crash together in bubbly hiccups.

Crabs strut in style with their pinchers held high,
In a salute to the surfers who zoom by.
They all gather round for an elegant dance,
Pincers clapping loudly, giving us a chance!

Waves giggle softly, tickling the shore,
While flip-flops gossip of life evermore.
The breeze carries tales of the day's crazy fun,
With laughter and joy, oh how we have won!

Where Water Meets the Shore

At the edge of the world where the sea starts to swoosh,
A sand crab named Pete does a funky little whoosh.
With a sideways shimmy and a cheeky grin,
He dances with shells, inviting all to begin!

The waves wash in secrets and tickle your feet,
While clams gossip softly, isn't life sweet?
Seashells are trumpets, announcing their reign,
As dolphins make waves in the fishy campaign.

A pelican named Mel, with a beak full of charms,
Flies over beach umbrellas, with grace and with arms.
He drops off a fish with a wink and a quack,
Leaving beachgoers laughing, he makes quite the pack!

Mermaids are giggling in bubbles of glee,
Playing tic-tac-toe with the fish and the sea.
The foamy waves laugh, creating a show,
Where antics abound, let's all join the flow!

Riddles of the Nautilus Shell

Inside a shell home, where the wise one resides,
A nautilus chuckles, in circles he glides.
With riddles and laughter that spirals on out,
He spins tales of tides, oh what a loud shout!

He twirls like a dancer, a conch in his hand,
Crafting up stories like castles in sand.
"Why did the barnacle wed the old ship?" he beams,
"Because love is great, even covered in creams!"

With colors of rainbows and jokes to unfold,
He welcomes the fish, with adventures so bold.
"Why do the waves never play hide and seek?"
"Because they're too busy with laughter each week!"

So gather your friends, join a whirl in the shell,
Where wisdom is funny and stories compel.
In the whirlpool of laughter, the currents do tell,
The ocean's great wonders, it does very well!

www.ingramcontent.com/pod-product-compliance
Lightning Source LLC
Chambersburg PA
CBHW051733290426
43661CB00123B/249